Boards and More

Written by Linda Cave

Saturday morning I was going to the park. I had my new soccer ball with me. Soccer is my favorite sport. Before I could go, Dad stopped me.

"Mark, let's go to the store," he said.

"Is this going to be boring?" I asked.

"You'll see," Dad said.

Dad started the car. He was smiling and happy. "How far is it to the store?" I asked.

"It's a short trip," said Dad.

At last we got to the store. It was busy and very large. Dad was humming.

We parked the car and went inside. "Let's get a cart," said Dad. "Then we can start to shop."

I saw all sorts of stuff. This store was not boring at all. It was fun to explore.

Dad and I stopped the cart. We looked at hammers and saws and other tools. Dad chose a new power saw. He got a sawhorse to go with it.

"What are you going to build?" I asked.

"You mean what are WE going to build," said Dad. "You will have to guess!"

"We need some hardware," said Dad.

"You have lots of nails in jars at home," I said.

"But I need more," said Dad. "Can you guess what we are going to build?"

"No, not yet," I said.

Next we went to get some lumber. "Hold out your arms," said Dad. He placed a short board on them.

"We will need some long boards, too," he added. "Can you guess what we are going to build?"

"No, I still don't know," I said.

Dad ordered the long boards. A man at the store helped us load all the lumber.

"NOW can you guess what we are going to build?" Dad asked.

"Let's see," I said. "We have lumber, a saw, a sawhorse, and nails. I think I know what we are going to build!"

"We are going to build a fort for me!"